Mr. McD
and His Scooter

Written by Jill Eggleton
Illustrated by Richard Hoit

Mr. McDoodle
bought a scooter.
It was orange and purple
and silver and green.

"Can you ride it?"
asked the salesperson.

And Mr. McDoodle said,

"How
preposterous!

I can ride a scooter
like a surfer rides a wave."

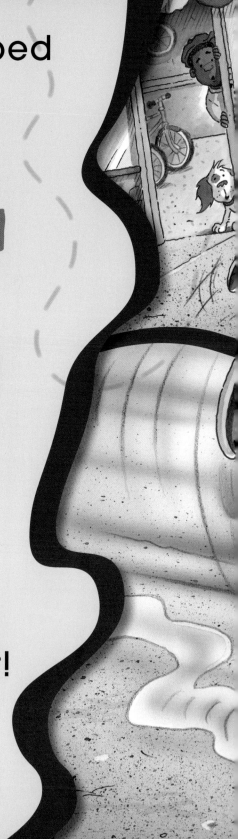

Mr. McDoodle leaped
on the scooter.

And off he went . . .

wibbling and
wobbling
and weaving
down the
Street.

Faster and faster
and faster
went his feet!

But Mr. McDoodle
went too fast.
He crashed
into a trash can!
Over went the
trash can!

Who – oo – osh went
the trash and . . .

thump, thud
went Mr. McDoodle.

"Botheration!"

he said.

A woman helped
Mr. McDoodle up.
"Can you ride this scooter?"
asked the woman.

Mr. McDoodle said,
"How preposterous!

I can ride this scooter
like a surfer rides a wave."

8

Mr. McDoodle leaped
on the scooter.

And off he went . . .

wibbling and
wobbling
and weaving
down the
Street.

Faster and faster
and faster
went his feet!

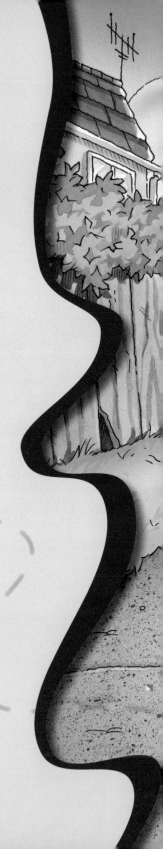

But Mr. McDoodle
went too fast.
He crashed
into a fruit stand.
Over went the
fruit stand!

Splat went
the fruit and . . .

thump, thud
went Mr. McDoodle.

"Botheration!"

he said.

A boy helped
Mr. McDoodle up.
"Can you ride this scooter?"
he asked.

Mr. McDoodle said,

"How preposterous!

I can ride this scooter
like a surfer rides a wave!"

14

Mr. McDoodle leaped on the scooter.

And off he went . . . wibbling and wobbling and weaving down the street.

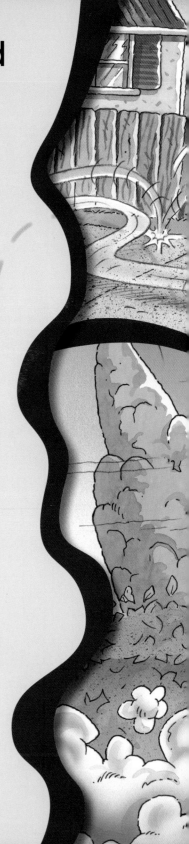

Faster and faster
and faster
went his feet!

But Mr. McDoodle
crashed into a table –
thump, thud and . . .

into a pole –
thump, thud and . . .

into a flower stand –
thump, thud and . . .

into a hole –
thump, thud!

**"Botheration! Botheration!
Botheration!"**
said Mr. McDoodle.
"I **can't** ride this scooter."

So Mr. McDoodle went to Scooter School, and he learned to ride that scooter!

Now Mr. McDoodle goes . . .

whirling and
twirling
and twisting
down the
Street.

Faster and faster
and faster
go his feet!

And everyone says,
"That Mr. McDoodle
can ride a scooter
like a surfer rides a wave."

Guide Notes

Title: **Mr. McDoodle and His Scooter**
Stage: Grade 2

Genre: Fiction
Approach: Shared Reading
Processes: Thinking Critically, Exploring Language,
   Processing Information
Written and Visual Focus: Change of Text Style,
   Illustrative Text

THINKING CRITICALLY
(sample questions)
- Why do you think Mr. McDoodle wanted a scooter?
- Why do you think people kept asking Mr. McDoodle if he could ride the scooter?
- Why do you think Mr. McDoodle couldn't ride the scooter?
- What do you think Mr. McDoodle might have learned at Scooter School?
- What do you think is meant when "Mr. McDoodle can ride a scooter like a surfer rides a wave" is mentioned in the text?
- Do you think this story could be true? Why/Why not?

EXPLORING LANGUAGE

Terminology
Title, cover, illustrations, author, illustrator

Vocabulary
Interest words: preposterous, wibbling, wobbling, weaving, botheration, whirling, twirling, twisting, splat, thump, thud
Contractions: can't
Compound words: salesperson, into, everyone
Singular/Plurals: scooter/scooters, feet/foot, surfer/surfers, school/schools, person/people
Antonyms: faster/slower, can't/can, ride/walk, everyone/no-one
Homonyms: too/to, hole/whole
Synonyms: whirling/twirling/twisting, preposterous/ridiculous/silly, thump/bang

Print Conventions
Capital letter for sentence beginnings and names (**M**r. **M**cDoodle), periods, exclamation marks, quotation marks, commas, question marks, ellipses, apostrophes